THE SIX SENSES

IN A NUTSHELL

Demonstrated Transitions
from Bleak to Bold Narrative

Jessica Bell

Vine Leaves Press | Melbourne, Vic, Australia

THE SIX SENSES IN A NUTSHELL: DEMONSTRATED TRANSITIONS FROM BLEAK TO BOLD NARRATIVE

Copyright © 2013 Jessica Bell
All rights reserved.
ISBN-13: 0987593153
ISBN-10: 978-0-9875931-5-3

Published by Vine Leaves Press 2013
Melbourne, Vic, Australia

Cover Photography from Shutterstock.com
Cover design by Jessica Bell

ALSO BY JESSICA BELL

~ CONTENTS ~

~ INTRODUCTION ~

In the first two books in this series, I demonstrated the distinct difference between "telling" and "showing", and how you can turn those dreaded adverbs and clichés into exciting and unique imagery.

If you've read Books 1 and 2 of the *Writing in a Nutshell* series, you'll know that my own writing struggles led me to write these pocket-sized writing guides—so you can learn to hone your craft in bite-sized, manageable pieces. But let me reiterate something I said in Books 1 and 2, because I think it's very important to stress this: the purpose of this series is to inspire you to become better at your craft. To teach you how to grow as a writer. It will not *tell* you how to write. It will not preach writing rules and styles to you. But it will help you to realize that you *can*, little by little, end up with a brilliant piece of work.

I hope that this book—and if you've read all three, this series—inspires and motivates you to become a better writer. But please 'do not feel like you need to write like me. Everyone has their own style. Trying to write like somebody else is (bar writing exercises), in my opinion, the biggest disservice you can do for your work. So just remember: be yourself.

In this book, *The Six Senses in a Nutshell*, I show you how utilizing the six senses (*see, hear, smell, taste, touch,* and *instinct*) can really bring your writing to life. To do this successfully, you need to "show, not tell". Otherwise, these senses will not really be senses. The reader won't actually experience them, they will only "read about" them. And the whole point of reading a great book is to feel like you aren't actually reading. Right? Right. Using the six senses in an effective way will accomplish this.

The key to using sense in your writing, however, is to limit your use of the words, *see, feel, hear, smell* and *taste*. That's not to say you shouldn't ever use these words, but just be aware you don't overuse them.

The most ideal way to incorporate senses is to employ language in which sense is already a part of. For example, instead of saying *the kitchen smelled sweet with melted chocolate*, show the reader what's cooking, and consequently that taste and scent will be present in the narrative without you having to point it out.

Using the six senses well is also not only about having your *characters* sense things, it's about making your *readers* sense things—even elements that your characters aren't feeling, i.e., if the reader knows more than your character(s) do, or if you're showing something that you might react to differently than the characters in the book. You'll better understand what I mean when you read the eleven transitions in this book.

In each demonstrated transition I provide a BLEAK passage (prose lacking sensory information), and a BOLD passage (the BLEAK passage revamped to make it more appealing by utilizing sense in an indirect and/or stimulating way).

So, how should you use this book?

Step #1: Read through the BLEAK passage. Make notes on what senses it is lacking, or what senses could be added. Then, isolate each sentence. How would you revamp it to give it more life? (Your rewrite can extend beyond one sentence and include things that are not already present to make the scene more stimulating.) Before reading my BOLD passage, I want you to write your own. I've always believed a writer learns better by "doing", and then correcting the mistakes. That way you become more aware of the level of improvement you're making, and how you're making it.

Step #2: Put your BOLD attempt aside and read my BOLD passage. As you're reading, see if you can match the sentences you isolated in the BLEAK passage to any of the content in my BOLD passage. Briefly consider how the content has changed, developed, and acquired more life, but do not start analyzing it yet.

Step #3: Read through the WHICH SENSES HAVE BEEN USED AND HOW? section. I provide you with my own break down of the first sentence(s) of my BOLD passage, and tell you what senses have been used, and what/how they might make the reader feel. Remember, this is *my* interpretation of the content. We all know that every reader interprets what they read differently due to the influence of their own experiences. The key is to make people sense something, even if what they sense ends up being different to someone else. So don't feel let down if my interpretation is different to yours—you didn't do anything wrong. We are all unique individuals. Also note that when I use the word "feel" as a sense, I'm referring to both the physical (touch) and intuitive (sixth sense).

Step #4: Now mimic what I've done in the WHICH SENSES HAVE BEEN USED AND HOW? section, for the rest of my BOLD passage. Isolate each sentence of the text and write down which senses it utilizes and how.

Please note, however, that some sentences within a passage will not be overflowing with sensory information. Sometimes we need to break it up with simple transitional language to avoid sensory overload. This is why the examples in this book are lengthier than in *Show & Tell in a Nutshell*. I wanted to provide you with meatier text, but at the same time, not go too over the top.

Mind you, there also might be some passages that you feel are rife with what some people call "purple prose", i.e flowery language (Transition #1 for example). So I just want to make you aware that this is my literary/poetic style, and even though some people do not necessarily enjoy this style of writing, I think it's perfect for illustrating the point I'm making with this book.

Step #5: Look at your own attempt at the BLEAK passage. Now improve it.

Step #6: After you've been through the eleven transitions, look at the WHAT NOW? section at the end of the book, where there is an additional writing exercise.

By following these steps, I hope you will be inspired to transform the bleak into bold. Remember, just be yourself. And please don't feel ashamed to write in this book. It's what it's made for.

Note: You'll notice that this book doesn't have an index. That's because if I included one, it would give away all the answers and contaminate your own interpretation of the texts.

Happy writing!

Why 11 transitions, and not an even 10 or 12? Because in numerology, it is a Master Number and represents intuition, which is the sixth sense. Fitting, yes?

TRANSITION #1

BLEAK

The island is very beautiful, extremely hot, and all the houses are white with colourful wooden windows. In the mornings, it can get very noisy too, especially with all the insects and animals left free to roam wherever they like. And the bread truck makes a decent amount of racket. But it's so wonderful how people get their bread delivered. Beats going to the supermarket, that's for sure. I think the people that live there are a bit weird though—they give me the creeps for some reason. But I do love living on this island because it's very relaxing. And when the heat gets too much to handle, all you have to do is jump into the sea to cool off. It's absolute bliss!

BOLD

The island's windy mountainous roads are framed with olive groves and air so crisp you could snap it like celery. The houses are stained with whitewash and embedded with old-style wooden shutters, tailored by the locals to keep the summer swelter out. They are painted blue, red, or green, but occasionally you may come across the odd pink or orange shutters, which are more often than not inhabited by the eccentric barmy type who are colour-blind, or the young and loaded foreigner who believes an island revolution should be in order.

Goats meander about the streets, butting each other's heads senselessly as they try to escape oncoming cars and motorcycles. The roosters, chickens, and geese fire up the locals at the first sign of sunrise. Birds chirp, cicadas "jijiga" in the olive trees, and dogs bark as the bread truck, a red beat-up Ute, delivers fresh hot loaves to each residence, and slips the required amount of bread into handmade cloth bags hanging from wire fencing.

Summer on this island engraves your skin with a longing to spend sunrise to sunset lying on a small, empty, white-pebbled beach in a secluded cove at the end of a private dirt track. At midday, it gets so hot you need to wade through the heat waves rising from the uneven tarred road like kindred spirits before you can wade in the Ionian Sea to cool off—a flat, motionless oil bath which glows with an infinite turquoise glint. It may seem you are stepping into velvet, however, you emerge covered in a thin salty crust you can brush off like sand when it dries.

WHICH SENSES HAVE BEEN USED AND HOW?

Let me get you started …

See, Feel, Smell/Taste ~ "The island's windy mountainous roads are framed with olive groves and air so crisp you could snap it like celery."

What can you see? Vast green, olive trees, windy roads, steep hills

What can you feel? A fresh breeze brush against my skin. It's not actually written, but it's there between the lines.

What can you smell or taste? Fresh crisp celery, which denotes the feeling of fresh air, and perhaps a little condensation

Read the BOLD example again. Isolate each sentence and identify what senses are being utilized, and how.

~NOTES~

TRANSITION #2

BLEAK

The sun shone through the window. The living room was dusty and the furniture was in the same place it had always been for the previous twenty-five years. The interior design was ancient, and looked as depressed as the people who lived there, including Fran.

Fran watched TV commercials with the volume down—everyone and everything looked fake and overcompensated. It almost made her feel ashamed to be Australian.

The crickets were making a lot of noise. So were all the appliances in the kitchen.

Everything was so loud.

And so monotonous.

Fran had to get out of there.

BOLD

The sun bled an orange glucose shard of light through the dusty blinds. Thick dust layered the TV screen, no longer camouflaged by the night. For Fran's entire life, the TV had sat in this exact position. In the corner. On a mahogany treasure chest with an intricately designed rusty metal latch. Not once in her twenty-five years had the furniture been moved around. She couldn't even remember the rug under the coffee table being removed, or steam-cleaned. But somehow everything had remained tidy, soulless, covered by an invisible sheen of emotional filth. A happy homemaker's cocoon inhabited by the manically depressed who succeeded in making others believe they were perfectly fine. Fran was not an exception.

Fran watched commercials in mute— graceful images of happy blonde, blue-eyed nuclear families eating Vegemite sandwiches in abnormally green and large grassy backyards. Images of zealous teens throwing Frisbees and rubber balls for golden retrievers that didn't need to be given orders, and of dogs herding sheep like obedient robots. Of young, outrageously cute crystal-eyed siblings hugging and kissing each other, as if they'd never thrown tantrums over toy-snatching. Of parents looking impossibly content, barbequing up a feast for their statistically calculated 2.5 kids, under an fake cloudless sky. All in all, a stereotypical view of Australia, distorted by blank sound, with raging lawn mowers as backdrop.

The crickets had just begun their nightly symphonic orchestra. The fridge shuddered. The water filter bubbled. The clock ticked. The kitchen tap dripped ... waste-ing-wor-tah.

I'm going to go mad if I don't leave, Fran thought.

WHICH SENSES HAVE BEEN USED AND HOW?

Let me get you started …

See, Feel, Smell ~ "The sun bled an orange glucose shard of light through the dusty blinds."

What can you see? Dim orange sun light, dust in the air, window with blinds slightly open

What can you feel? Warm, yet stuffy and downbeat, perhaps a tickly nose from the dust

What can you smell? A musty room, yet slightly sweet; the impression that the air is thick and oppressive

Read the BOLD example again. Isolate each sentence and identify what senses are being utilized, and how.

~NOTES~

TRANSITION #3

BLEAK

Nelly feels so drunk and dizzy from all the visual and aural stimulation in this night club that she thinks she might soon throw up.

"Darling, I think we'd better get you home," Hans says, helping her up. "Can you walk?"

"Um … yep." Nelly stands, and pretends to be fine. She'll be glad to get a breath of air after being so long in that stuffy club.

Out on the street, the cold air somewhat revitalizes her senses. When her cell vibrates in her handbag, Hans makes a sarcastic remark about her shock. Nelly sighs at the ridiculous hour she's receiving a call and almost loses balance searching her bag for the phone.

"Hello?"

"Oh good, I haven't woken you up. I had a feeling you'd be out and about."

"What do you want?"

"I might be close to finding Dan."

Dan? What?

"But I don't want to see Dan. I hate the bastard. You know that! Why would you even bother, Carol?"

Nelly and Carol end up arguing and hanging up on bad terms. But Nelly suddenly feels awful about the way she spoke to her and is afraid she may have lost her only true friend.

BOLD

Nelly looks up at Hans's wavering foggy face and the tri-image of the large TV screen of the Pet Shop Boys' *Absolutely Fabulous* video clip pounding on the large screen overhead. Her body convulses forward and she cups a hand to her mouth, stunting the vomit in its tracks.

"Darling, I think we'd better get you home."

Nelly nods, managing to keep the spew at bay. Hans grabs Nelly's bag and helps her to stand. "Can you walk?"

"Um ... yep." She stands, holds her head high, straightens her silver spandex boob tube above her breasts, and fakes it. At least until they get out of the claustrophobic, and overly smoke-machined atmosphere where she can take a nice deep breath.

Out on the street, waiting for a cab, the sharp early morning air cuts right through her, bringing her senses back to life and turning her entertaining drunken dizziness and drugged bounce into a sick whirlpool of indignation. The sounds of cars on wet roads *whoosh* through her ears as if she's listening to panned sound effects through headphones. She clutches her handbag under her arm when the ground starts to pulsate. She looks at Hans as if something is sawing her in half.

"Honey," Hans says, lighting a cigarette, "death isn't embedded into your side. It's your cell. Vibrating."

Nelly loosens her grip and sighs in relief. She searches her bag for the phone.

"What the hell time is it? 4:00 a.m.?" Nelly rolls her eyes at Hans. He chuckles when she almost loses balance and starts to walk backward. She grabs the phone, stops in the middle of the sidewalk holding one arm out to her side as if ready to launch into flight.

"Hello?"

"Oh good, I haven't woken you. I had a feeling you'd be out and about."

"Carol. Why are you doing calling me so late?"

"What's wrong? You're awake, aren't you?"

"What do you want?"

"I might be close to finding Dan."

Nelly pulls the phone away from her ear and glares at the keypad as if it has a voice of its own. She looks at Hans who shrugs in question. She puts the phone back to her ear.

"What the hell?"

"Yeah, I know. After all these years. Come home. Let's try and meet up with him together?"

"Don't be ridiculous, Carol. Why on earth would I want to do that for? I'm finally getting my shit together."

"I'm discovering some serious stuff, Nelly, and I think you should be here. I think we should do this together."

Nelly coughs in disgust as if Carol's request has regurgitated bile.

"Carol, I don't know what kind of world you're living in, but it's not mine. Okay? I don't give a damn about Dan or about any of the 'serious shit' you're finding out. Let me live my life, and you live yours. Maybe you can try to do that on your own for once too, huh? Or would you like me to hire someone to hold your hand now that I'm not around anymore?"

Nelly cringes at Carol's quick inward breath as if trying to ignore the hurt.

"But don't you want to know what happened to him?"

Nelly closes her eyes. Remembers the time he left her for dead in a ditch ...

"I don't care. Plus, I've already caught up with him and told him to never contact me again."

"You what?"

Silence thickens in Nelly's ear.

"How could you not ..."

"Say anything? Oh, I don't know. Maybe because some people don't talk about things simply because they don't want crap in their lives. Maybe because my life is *mine*, and I can do what *I* like with it? Got it?"

"But, I thought we … loved each other," Carol gurgles. "I thought we were a team. I thought we agreed to seek revenge. Together."

"Grow up, Carol. Things change."

Carol sobs. A pinch of pain expands in Nelly's stomach like a chemical contamination, swelling, gushing through her mouth in torrents. "Stop calling me. Learn to live without me. Our whole family should be fed to the wolves."

Nelly hangs up the phone and throws it in her bag. She lifts her head, her mind and body flooded with freedom and guilty triumph, to see Hans's hand cupped over his mouth, and tears streaming down his cheeks. At this moment, she realizes, she has just pushed away the only person in the world she unconditionally loves. And that she may never be able to get her back.

WHICH SENSES HAVE BEEN USED AND HOW?

Let me get you started …

See, Feel, Taste, Hear ~ "Nelly looks up at Hans's wavering foggy face and the tri-image of the large TV screen of the Pet Shop Boys' *Absolutely Fabulous* video clip pounding on the large screen overhead. Her body convulses forward and she cups a hand to her mouth, stunting a vomit warning in its tracks."

What can you see? A blurry vision of a person's face and video clip

What can you feel? Dizziness, nausea

What can you taste? Alcohol, vomit

What can you hear? Loud music

*Read the **BOLD** example again. Isolate each sentence and identify what senses are being utilized, and how.*

~NOTES~

~NOTES~

TRANSITION #4

BLEAK

As soon as Samantha arrived home a gusty wind started up. She looked at the small garden she'd attempted to landscape the previous year and was reminded of how she had failed to keep it alive. Except for one stubborn lemon tree. She felt like such a disappointment that even the brass lion-head knocker on her front door seemed to mock her.

She didn't want to go inside. Especially since *he* was home. She could hear him playing computer games. The sound of cars, and his frustration, came wafting out the open window. Suddenly he switched off the game.

Samantha quietly stepped inside and left her briefcase by the door hoping her son might get nosey, take a peek inside, and find her journal.

She felt uneasy, but tried not to let it show as she headed to the kitchen where her son seemed to be scouring for food in the fridge. And behaving like a pig. As usual.

"What's up, Mark?"

Mark made a rude gesture and walked out without uttering a word.

"Don't you just walk away from me," Samantha yelled. "You come back and apologize."

Samantha sat at the kitchen table and looked around. The place was a pigsty and smelled like someone had thrown up their dessert.

As Mark locked himself in his room and turned his music on at full volume, she realized how trapped she felt in her own home.

BOLD

The wind blew Samantha's blouse flat against her back as she scanned the overgrown section of grass where she'd attempted to landscape a mini rock garden last year. The pile of decorative pebbles were now lost in weeds, and fermenting apricots. The tiny lemon tree even struggled to survive on its own, producing one lemon a year, as if too stubborn to be conquered by human neglect.

Samantha stood on her doorstep, briefcase in hand, staring at the brass lion head knocker. Every time she returned home, she was sure she could hear the lion spitting at her: *You never learn, do you woman?*

She didn't want to go inside. She never wanted to go inside. He'd be waiting for her, ready to pounce, either with degrading comments or silence; she didn't know which one was worse. But she's got to stop doing this. Working late every night wouldn't fix the relationship between them. It wouldn't fix *him*.

As she inserted her key, the sound of a car screeching and crashing leaped from the open living room window. He'd left the fly-wire off. Again.

Something fell to the floor and thick thuds followed—a bit of bookcase abuse, perhaps. The roar of the digital explosion stopped abruptly. Perhaps he'd turned off the TV.

She opened the door slow enough for the hinges not to squeak and stepped inside, placed her briefcase delicately by the door as she did every night—easy access for the following morning. No. The real reason was because she hoped her son would open it and read the journal she left in there. The one that's all about her struggles coping with him. Maybe he'd feel sorry for her and realize how manipulative he was.

Samantha took a deep breath, adjusted the cuffs and collar of her blouse, pushed her hair behind her ears and rubbed her chapped lips together.

She strode down the hallway, head high, toward the kitchen at the other end. Her son's shadow rippled over the tiled floor as she approached the arched entrance way. The fridge door opened and closed. Its contents rattled like the music of water-filled crystal glasses. Along with a running bath, it was perhaps the only other relaxing sound she ever heard in this household.

Her son scoffed, snorted, coughed, spat into the sink. Samantha could hear it splatter like fresh fish gut. She leaned against the archway, folded her arms under her breasts, and tried to drill a hole through his head with her glare.

"What's up, Mark?" Samantha raised her eyebrows, trying to maintain assertion.

Mark looked up and smirked, shoved a hand down the front of his jeans and rearranged his package. Samantha scanned him up and down in disgust. Mark winked, spat into the sink again, and walked out without uttering a word.

"Don't you just walk away from me," Samantha called toward the ceiling, trying to disguise her tears with volume. "You come back and apologize."

Samantha pulled out a chair and sat at the kitchen table. The counter and sink overflowed with dirty dishes. And there was something pink and sticky, cough syrup perhaps, all over the floor by the dishwasher, and brown broken glass at the base of the garbage bin.

Samantha jumped in her seat as Mark's bedroom door slammed and the boom of heavy metal sucked the oxygen right out of the air.

This was a prison.

And she'd built it herself.

WHICH SENSES HAVE BEEN USED AND HOW?

Let me get you started …

See, Feel, Hear, Smell ~ "The wind blows Samantha's blouse flat against her back as she looks at the round overgrown patch of grass where she attempted to landscape a mini rock garden last year."

What can you see? Samantha's garden that leaves a lot to be desired

What can you feel? Strong wind, the silky material of a blouse brush against skin

What can you hear? Wind, leaves rustling

What can you smell? Grass, perhaps dead flowers/plants/weeds.

Read the BOLD example again. Isolate each sentence and identify what senses are being utilized, and how.

~NOTES~

TRANSITION #5

BLEAK

While Gary lies on his back on the grass by the river the noises of the city surround him.

He closes his eyes, flicks his cigarette in the river and tries not to feel guilty about polluting the earth. What difference is one cigarette going to make anyway?

He screams his testament to the sky and finally—finally—he cries and releases his stress.

BOLD

Gary doesn't move from his position on
the grass by the river—flat on his back. He
closes his eyes. Cyclists' chains clink as
they glide by his head; cars rumble on the
bridge behind him; leaves rustle in the
wind. The sun disappears. Thunder
cracks. Rain pelts down.

He flicks his cigarette toward the river
knowing it won't even make it close. This
time he doesn't feel guilty. The river is
brown. City brown shit pollution crap,
what-the-hell-are-we-doing-wrong *brown*.

What's one more fag?

What's one more sorry broken soul taking
his stress out on the river?

What difference does it make?

"What difference does it bloody make?" he roars, punching both fists and feet repeatedly toward the sky.

And then it finally happens with one huge breath of wet air.

He cries.

He cries, and his body trembles against the earth.

WHICH SENSES HAVE BEEN USED AND HOW?

Let me get you started …

See, Feel, Hear, Smell ~ "Gary doesn't move from his position on the grass by the river—flat on his back. He closes his eyes. Cyclists' chains clink as they glide by his head; cars rumble on the bridge behind him; leaves rustle in the wind."

What can you see? The sky, and then pitch black

What can you feel? Grass, wind

What can you hear? The river, bicycles and cars in motion, rustling leaves

What can you smell? City smog, grass, perhaps the river if you envision one that is polluted

Read the BOLD example again. Isolate each sentence and identify what senses are being utilized, and how.

~ NOTES ~

TRANSITION #6

BLEAK

Joe sits down for his morning coffee, tobacco and papers in front of the TV, and wishes his daughter Sandra would just go on a diet already.

He goes through the motions of pinching the tobacco and rolling the paper as he waits for Sandra to finish in the kitchen. He holds it up to the light and admires his handiwork.

Sandra finally comes and sits down next to him and takes the cigarette out of Joe's fingers. Joe watches her light it, and smoke it all in almost one breath.

Joe looks at Sandra with pity and hopes that she listens to his advice before it's too late. He'll always love her no matter what she looks like. But he also wants her to love herself.

BOLD

Joe switches the channel one last time, leans over the coffee table, sips his double espresso, and gathers his packet of Drum, filters, papers, to roll a few cigs. He can sense Sandra's laser-like stare from behind the kitchen counter as he lodges the first rollie behind his right ear. She's urging him to let her off the hook. But he won't give in again. For the sake of her health, if anything. What kind of father would he be if he didn't put his foot down once in a while?

"Another week. And you won't feel so hungry."

Joe listens to the steadiness of his breath, watches as his calloused and bitten fingertips pinch tobacco into a neat line across the paper as though a different brain were giving his hands the orders. He rolls the tobacco between his thumbs and forefingers, licks the edge of the paper, seals it into a perfect silky cylinder. Without looking up from the coffee table, he holds the cigarette in the air.

Sandra drags her heavy feet across the carpet. A sound Joe associates with the Rottweiler they had when his ex-wife was still around.

Sandra snatches the cigarette and sits next to Joe. The leather couch sinks with a sigh. He turns to her, head still hanging, tilted to the side. She lights the cigarette with a match from her black polo shirt pocket. With only one drag, half of it disappears. Joe scrutinizes Sandra's puffy cheeks and baby-like fat that's starting to form a double chin. He still thinks she's cute. But if she keeps going like this he's worried he'll start to find his own daughter ugly. His throat tightens and he squints at her before kissing her forehead.

WHICH SENSES HAVE BEEN USED AND HOW?

Let me get you started ...

See, Feel, Taste, Hear, Smell ~ "Joe switches the channel one last time, leans over the coffee table, sips his double espresso, and gathers his packet of Drum, filters, papers, to roll a few cigs."

What can you see? TV, coffee table, coffee, cigarette papers, tobacco

What can you feel? Cigarette/papers/filters packets, handle of the espresso cup; perhaps boredom and/or morning blues?

What can you taste? Coffee, tobacco

What can you hear? Voices from the TV

What can you smell? Coffee, tobacco

Read the BOLD example again. Isolate each sentence and identify what senses are being utilized, and how.

~NOTES~

TRANSITION #7

BLEAK

I've just come home from the beach. I
stand outside our apartment for a while,
enjoying a sense of newfound freedom.

When I enter, my daughter Molly and our
new puppy dog run toward me and I pat
and hug them. It's such a lovely moment
of happiness that I wish I could be in it
forever.

My husband, Tom, is at his desk, trying
not to show any emotion. I hesitantly walk
over to him, despite not wanting to. I give
him a quick kiss regardless.

"What's up?" Tom must think I've given
in.

I tell him that I missed him but that it
doesn't mean that everything is okay
between us. Oh, how I wish we could turn
back time and be happily married again.

He notices that my shirt has become see-through from my wet bathing suit. Once upon a time it would have been a turn on, but instead, he looks at me in disgust.

BOLD

I stand in the hallway outside our apartment, sea salt burning a small cut in my nose. I hold my shirt sleeve against it with my wrist, trying to sooth the sting—my handbag falls down around my elbow. My hair partly dry, stuck together in clumps like dreadlocks, tickles the back of my neck. Like a birthmark, the scent of ocean owns me. Smells like ... freedom? Salt grains exfoliating pollution from my skin.

I open the door and Molly and our puppy come charging for me like bulls. Molly clutches the puppy's left ear. The puppy pants, her thick pink bouncy tongue hanging from the side of her mouth. I kneel down and hug them both at once. Drool splashes on my hand. I intend to scratch her behind her ears, and stroke Molly's hair, but my wires get crossed and I do the reverse. I wish the three of us could sit on the floor in the corridor all night—in a cocoon of unconditional love, freedom from the world, no responsibility, no ache, simple pleasure at its best.

My husband, Tom, is at his desk, blank-faced. I walk over to him, unsure of what to say, whether I want to say anything at all, or even if I want to be anywhere near him. I stand by his side. Don't utter a word. He doesn't look up. I bend down; semi-consciously give him a peck on the forehead.

"What's up?" Tom smirks as if I've given in. His voice snaps me back to reality.

"I missed you," I say, covering my bikini strap with my hair. "Doesn't mean I forgive you." I pull back. But I didn't miss him. I missed the idea of him; the impression of how we used to be.

He looks at my breasts through my damp shirt exposing blurred blue checks below.

Once upon a time he would have cupped his hands over them, squeezed them, and nudged me toward the bedroom. But now … he looks at them as if I'm violating some cultural indecent exposure law.

WHICH SENSES HAVE BEEN USED AND HOW?

Let me get you started ...

See, Feel, Taste, Smell ~ "I stand in the hallway outside our apartment, sea salt burning a small cut in my nose."

What can you see? The apartment door and hallway

What can you feel? Stinging inside nose, perhaps hesitant to go inside

What can you smell? Sea salt, the beach, maybe wet hair

Read the BOLD example again. Isolate each sentence and identify what senses are being utilized, and how.

~NOTES~

TRANSITION #8

BLEAK

I'm at the Hilton Hotel standing outside the lecture hall door observing all the pompous people in this building. And I'm nervous about giving this presentation. So nervous that I feel like throwing up. I need to stop fidgeting and get my shit together.

It's time. I walk into the lecture hall and stand behind the podium. I feel sweaty and I'm worried my nerves are radiating into the crowd. I can just feel I'm going to make a fool of myself.

Everyone turns to face me and I begin to shake and choke on the words I practiced to introduce myself.

I don't think this is going to go very well.

BOLD

At Hilton Hotel. Biting nails. Reciting presentation in head with the notes of guitar scales. Standing by lecture hall door, fingers twisted behind back, toes clenched in black baby doll flats. Changed shoes in the car. Watching freshly dry-cleaned suits, worn by impassive breathing corpses, walk by. Black pencil skirts and dusty patent leather high-heeled shoes on Stepford Wife splendor. Clop. Clop. Clopping. Past me like old slides. Bus boys with crisp white shirts and ugly yellow ties. Upper-class ladies in frilly blouses who eat with their mouths closed at all times, and wait for the thirty-second mouthful before swallowing, and pat their lips with expensive linen napkins.

A piece of nail gets lodged between my front teeth. I try to pry it out, exposing my teeth like a growling dog, but failing because I have no nails left to pry it out with. Middle-aged man in navy blue tailored trousers and pink shirt with collar opened three buttons down, grins at me in a ridiculing manner. His gold chain glistens amidst his thick dark chest hair as he passes below a chandelier. *Rich bastard. Trying to follow trends.* I bring my arms down to my sides and close my mouth, pushing the nail through my teeth with my tongue. Grimacing within, I smile back with my lips pressed together so tight I imagine them turning white.

I'm nauseous. Not because of presentation nerves, but because pink shirts make me want to vomit, for two reasons. One: they remind me of the time I was ten and put my white clothes in with the red bed sheets and mum pulled the heads off all my Barbie dolls as punishment. They also remind of when my husband got attacked by Greek rock venue mafia, and was left bleeding with a few knife gashes to his chest. White shirt stained with blood. Nothing serious. But what if it *had* been? I tried to scrub out the blood from his shirt by hand in the white porcelain bathroom sink. I'll never forget that feeling of infirmity spread from my feet, through my body, to the tip of my tongue. I had turned around and thrown up in the toilet bowl. Then continued to scrub, and had sung a stupid TV cheese jingle to distract myself from the overwhelming fear of what might happen next time.

It's time. I walk into the lecture hall and stand behind the podium. A bead of sweat tickles between my breasts. I want to scratch it. I grit my teeth trying to wane off the temptation, the air becoming a whirlwind of angst around my head. I cough into the microphone. Feedback. Feet shuffle. Voices murmur. Silence. A stray chuckle escapes from someone who was probably so preoccupied talking to the person next to them that they hadn't noticed I'd walked in.

Eyes focus on me as if I am an optometrist's letter chart. With shaking legs and a blank mind, I open my mouth to introduce myself, but words do not flee.

I'm screwed.

WHICH SENSES HAVE BEEN USED AND HOW?

Let me get you started ...

See, Feel, Taste, Hear ~ "At Hilton Hotel. Biting nails. Reciting presentation in head with the notes of guitar scales. Standing by lecture hall door, fingers twisted behind back, toes clenched in black baby doll flats."

What can you see? Interior of Hilton Hotel, a nervous woman

What can you feel? Nervous tension, nails between teeth, twisted fingers, clenched toes

What can you taste? Bitten nails

What can you hear? Guitar scales, inner voice reciting presentation, perhaps voices of people walking around hotel

Read the BOLD example again. Isolate each sentence and identify what senses are being utilized, and how.

~ NOTES ~

TRANSITION #9

BLEAK

Though he attempted to be quiet and not wake up Linda, Sean didn't quite manage it. He farted when he sat on the edge of the bed. He sat in still silence, hoping the smell wouldn't spread through the sheets. But Linda woke up and giggled. Yup, she could smell it all right. *Damn!*

"You should go back to sleep. It's only nine o'clock," Sean said, standing up and looking at himself in the mirror.

"What time did we go to sleep?" Linda asked sleepily.

Sean stood up and looked out the window at a woman fetching her morning paper— an unappealing picture of domesticity.

"Not sure, but I came over around half four."

Linda rolled over and went back to sleep.

Sean went into Linda's messy and disorganized kitchen to make a coffee to discover there was no coffee maker in sight or even milk in the fridge. The sight of the packed cardboard boxes in front of him made him feel like he was moving forward in this relationship too fast.

He returned to the bedroom. "Babe, do you have a percolator?"

"No. Just use the hot tap, or boil some water in the small pot on the stove. Everything else is packed away," Linda said.

Sean looked out the window again. Now the woman was arguing with her inattentive husband over the Christmas tree delivery.

"It's a sign," he thought.

He couldn't go through with this.

BOLD

Sean tried to sit on the edge of the bed without waking Linda. But failed miserably when his feet touched the carpet, and he accidentally let out a ripper of a fart. *Damn!* It bubbled behind his balls and sent dread through his chest. He stared at himself in the wardrobe mirror. *Maybe it's just loud because it's quiet in here.* He was afraid to move in case the smell spread through Linda's silky cotton sheets. His torso constricted; goose pimples formed around his nipples. Linda giggled and rubbed her eyes. *Shit. Can she smell it? I can smell it. Shit.* She nuzzled her face into her pillow and smudged makeup on it.

"Lovely," Linda croaked. "That's so much better than an alarm clock. Can you stay over during the week too?" She waved her hand in front of her nose.

"Sorry," Sean whispered.

"'S'not as bad as some I've experienced."

"You should go back to sleep. It's only nine o'clock," Sean said, standing and pulling on his boxers. He caught the reflection of his right bum cheek in the mirror. He had a huge hickey on it. *Are those teeth marks?*

"What time did we go to sleep?" Linda asked, struggling to open her eyes and shadowing them with her hand. She lifted both legs into the air and hooked the duvet underneath her feet.

Sean stood up straight, motionless, staring out the window at the grey wet street. He could see a lady fetching the Sunday paper in her pajamas and gumboots. She ripped the plastic off, pulled out the Christmas catalogues, and threw the newspaper in the street bin.

"Not sure, but I came around half four."

Linda grunted in agreement, rolled over, and pulled the covers over her head.

Sean stumbled into the kitchen to put on a pot of coffee. But he couldn't find the percolator. *Does she even have a percolator?* Crumbs crunched under his bare feet and got stuck between his toes. The kitchen bench was bare, and the pantry full of herbs, self-rising flour, canned minestrone soup, Jacob's instant coffee, and old jars of strawberry jam and Vegemite. There was one jar of Marmite too, still sealed. *That must be for emergencies.*

The inside of the fridge looked like a hospital ward in the midst of a bomb scare. There was a plate of moldy blueberry pancakes, a box of Chinese noodles with chopsticks and a fork still in it, and a couple of cans of Malibu and Coke. *No milk.* In the dish rack there sat one bowl, one mug, one soup spoon, and one teaspoon.

Packed cardboard boxes, sitting dormant next to the kitchen table against the wall, stared at Sean. They teased him, rubbing the fast-approaching and ambivalent future into his face.

He returned to the bedroom and pulled the covers from Linda's face. She smiled with her eyes shut, like a child who'd secretly eaten all the cake or drunk all the chocolate milk. Sean imagined her with a brown milky moustache.

"Babe, do you have a percolator?"

"No. Just use the hot tap, or boil some water in the small pot on the stove. Everything else is packed away," Linda said.

Sean didn't move. He looked out the window again. Now there was a truck delivering the woman a tree. She wore a heavy-looking coat over her pajamas this time. She pulled money out of her pocket and handed it to the delivery dude. Her husband ran out to help her drag the tree into the house. He was fully dressed and had his cell phone hooked between his ear and shoulder. The woman tripped, yelled something at her husband. He dropped the tree to the ground, held his finger up to his mouth to tell her to shoosh, and continued talking on his cell. She stamped her foot, threw her arms up in the air, and yelled something else before running back inside the house and slamming the front door.

The dread of another round of domesticity pricked at Sean's pores. *Ugh.*

WHICH SENSES HAVE BEEN USED AND HOW?

Let me get you started ...

See, Feel, Hear, Smell ~ "Sean tried to sit on the edge of the bed without waking Linda. But failed miserably when his feet touched the carpet, and he accidentally let out a ripper of a fart."

What can you see? A couple in bed, a carpeted bedroom

What can you feel? Feet on carpet, warm vibration of fart, tentative, apologetic, embarrassed

What can you hear? The fart, the quiet ruffle of bed sheets, the silence of morning

What can you smell? The fart, and perhaps morning breath

Read the BOLD example again. Isolate each sentence and identify what senses are being utilized, and how.

~NOTES~

TRANSITION #10

BLEAK

Betty's drunk mother, Kay, who's passed out on the couch, looks like she's been starved to death and beaten up. Everyone in their suburban neighborhood must think they are good-for-nothing lowlifes. Not only is the place tiny, but you can tell it's a dump just by looking in the backyard.

Betty noisily passes Kay to get to the kitchen—frankly, she couldn't give a damn if she woke her up.

As Kay wheezes, Betty looks at her disgusting, foul-smelling mother's body and wonders if she'll ever get over the guilt of wishing her dead.

BOLD

A bottle of Smirnoff lies on the floor, open, pleading next to Betty's mother, Kay, to wake up and take down its remaining drops with her morning cigarette. Kay's skeletal, feeble limbs are splayed in directions Betty recognizes as dead, bruised victims she's seen on Crime TV.

Their Australian suburban house is small—just slightly bigger than a caravan, but at least it doesn't have wheels—at least this means they're not quite 'trailer trash' despite what others may think.

Betty passes Kay to go into the kitchenette, being sure to make as much noise as possible—frankly, she couldn't give a damn if she woke Kay up; she'd probably take that last sip of vodka and pass out again anyway.

Kay is wheezing a little, so she's still alive
… so far. Betty wonders if she'll ever have
to face the inevitable time when 'passed
out' will have evolved to 'deceased.' If she
wishes for that day to come a lot sooner
than fate has planned, what will follow?
Devastation, or devastating relief? And if
the latter, will guilt wheedle its way into
every passing thought? Into her meals,
dress, makeup, false nails?

A glob of drool vibrates in the corner of
Kay's mouth with every breath of air that
struggles through her sticky cracked lips.
Strands of stiff bleach blonde hair,
clumped together and matted below her
ear, look petrified with dried saliva. Her
fingers twitch. She has two black nails
from when she jammed them in the hinge
of the alcohol cabinet door. She groans.
One eye opens. Betty stares right at it—a
vibrant crystal blue bordered with a
yellowy, bloodshot white.

WHICH SENSES HAVE BEEN USED AND HOW?

Let me get you started ...

See, Feel, Smell ~ "A bottle of Smirnoff lies on the floor, open, pleading for Betty's mother, Kay, to wake up and take down its remaining drops with her morning cigarette."

What can you see? A daughter looking at her alcoholic mother passed out on the floor.

What can you feel? Pity, or perhaps disgust

What can you smell? Stale alcohol, stale cigarette smoke

Read the BOLD example again. Isolate each sentence and identify what senses are being utilized, and how.

~NOTES~

TRANSITION #11

BLEAK

I gaze up at the Acropolis in Athens, Greece, and I'm in awe of its ancient beauty.

Climbing to the top is difficult with my four-year-old daughter, Carla, in a wheelchair, but I manage to get her as far as the entrance—it's going to be a tough climb to the top as it's still quite hot for September. I'll need to find some help.

To my surprise, a little old lady offers the perfect solution. She gives me her scarf and fixes it around my neck like a big sling Carla can sit in.

I'm so appreciative of her help that I buy her something to eat and drink while she waits for us to return.

"Thanks so much. We won't be long," I say, nodding and smiling as we begin the climb.

BOLD

I gaze at the Acropolis in Athens, Greece. The air, marinated with late Cretaceous limestone dust that once accommodated the feet of countless ancient civilians, caresses my cheeks. The grounds are bristled with tufts of dry and newly sprouting grass, and scattered with rock shavings, large, small, and just plain humungous. A thick film of beige dust has settled over the entire area, and I can't help but wonder, when I rub it between my fingers, whether I am touching the remains of a Greek God or Goddess.

Climbing to the top along the slippery cobblestone path proves to be difficult with my four-year-old daughter, Carla, in a wheelchair, but I manage to get her as far as the entrance, where the wide but bumpy road ends, and the stairway to heaven begins—a stairway, I now wish Carla could walk up herself.

Shading my face with my right hand from the scorching early September sun, I scan for women tourists.

Perhaps someone has a child carrier Carla could fit in.

To my surprise, a short, plump old lady, wearing white sneakers and black widow's attire, taps me on the shoulder and says in English with a gentle Greek accent, "You want take child, I take wheelchair. I wait here, yes?" She removes her long black scarf from around her head and ties it around my neck and shoulder like a handbag. "This will help, *agapi mou*. She can sit, like chair. See?" She pushes her hands into the scarf to open it up.

Stunned by her kindness, all I immediately manage is an ebullient nod and smile.

"Thank you. Thank you, so much," I say, brainstorming how to demonstrate my appreciation. "Um, wait. One moment."

I dash to the kiosk and buy the lady a cheese pie and bottle of water. The lady takes a seat in Carla's wheelchair, and a hearty bite out of her pie, then holds it in the air as if toasting a glass of wine. Nodding and smacking her lips together, she says, "I wait here. You no worry. You *no* worry, *agapi mou.* Go. Go see brilliant structure." A flake of pastry drops off the pie and onto her chin as she takes another bite. A protruding skin-coloured mole secures it in position as she nods again in thanks.

"Thanks so much. We won't be long," I say, nodding and smiling in gratitude as we begin the daunting climb.

WHICH SENSES HAVE BEEN USED AND HOW?

Let me get you started …

See, Feel, Hear, Smell ~ "I gaze at the Acropolis in Athens, Greece. The air, marinated with late Cretaceous limestone dust that once accommodated the feet of countless ancient civilians, caresses my cheeks."

What can you see? The Acropolis, limestone, dust, and perhaps bare-footed ancient Greeks in Roman style clothing

What can you feel? A sense of magic, a soft breeze on my cheeks

What can you hear? Perhaps background chatter, shuffling feet

What can you smell? The dust of dry rock, and perhaps Athens city pollution

Read the BOLD example again. Isolate each sentence and identify what senses are being utilized, and how.

NOW WHAT?

For the sake of practice, let's say that all the BOLD passages were written by you. Let's say that each one is a vignette (a written snapshot) that a literary journal wishes to publish, but in order for them to be published, they require you cut their length down by half.

In each WHICH SENSES HAVE BEEN USED AND HOW? section, I asked you to isolate each sentence of the BOLD passages and identify what senses are being utilized, and how. Refer to those lists and rewrite the BOLD passages using half as many words, but still using all the senses you listed.

When you're done, choose your best one and email it to me! I'd love to read it.

To email me your rewrites, please do so via the contact form on my website: www.jessicabellauthor.com

~NOTES~

~NOTES~

~NOTES~

~NOTES~

~NOTES~

~NOTES~

~NOTES~

~NOTES~

ABOUT THE AUTHOR

If Jessica Bell could choose only one creative mentor, she'd give the role to Euterpe, the Greek muse of music and lyrics. This is not only because she currently resides in Athens, Greece, but because of her life as a thirty-something Australian-native contemporary fiction author, poet and singer/songwriter/guitarist, whose literary inspiration often stems from songs she's written.

Jessica is the Co-Publishing Editor of *Vine Leaves Literary Journal* and the director of the Homeric Writers' Retreat & Workshop on the Greek island of Ithaca. She makes a living as a writer/editor for English Language Teaching Publishers worldwide, such as Pearson Education, HarperCollins, MacMillan Education, Education First and Cengage Learning.

Visit her website:
www.jessicabellauthor.com

BOOK #1 FROM THE *WRITING IN A NUTSHELL SERIES*:

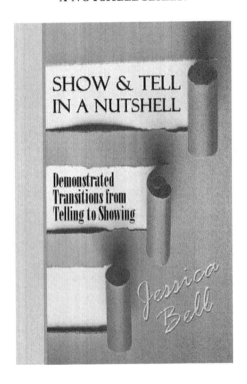

Reader reviews from Amazon for *Show & Tell in a Nutshell*:

"Simple, friendly, and applicable. Went back to my finished novel and observed some holes I should take care of next time. I've read a lot about the 'show-don't-tell' mystery. But this book hit home. The approach makes dull narratives come alive."

"Bell's brilliant nuts-and-bolts examples provide just what every writer needs to not only understand the concept, but to implement it. Know why? She doesn't just tell us about this concept... she shows us. Kinda fitting, dontcha think?"

"I could not believe the amount of scenes Jessica managed to create with such flair and intensity. The tone of each was so very different. I have never seen such obvious yet beautiful examples of showing. As an editor, I look forward to recommending this book to my authors. It has the ability to broaden a writer's horizon not just in showing but in the tone and temper used."

"To make action scenes and characters come alive, you show instead of tell. With sixteen examples of show versus tell and writing exercises at the end, SHOW & TELL IN A NUTSHELL is a fantastic resource for writers. If someone has had agents, editors, critique partners, and so on point out areas of telling—which is a weakness—this book will help strengthen his or her writing."

"I didn't hunt this book down. It was recommended to me, so I snatched it up immediately after reading the blurb. When I read Bell's introduction it was like looking in a mirror. I've been critiqued on occasion for having produced too much telling and not enough showing in my fictional works. I nearly gave up the search for a concise and practical set of tools like the ones Bell offers in her quick to read, easy to use manual. I now have a new found confidence to get back to working on revising one of my works in progress, using the techniques I've picked up by reading "Show & Tell In A Nutshell." Thanks Ms. Bell for doing such a great job making the concept so accessible."

BOOK #2 FROM THE *WRITING IN A NUTSHELL SERIES*:

Reader reviews from Amazon for
Adverbs & Clichés in a Nutshell:

"I love the structure of this book. Its quick and to-the-point examples are genius and so easy to follow, very user-friendly. Throughout her examples, Bell challenges the writer to see these flaws in his/her writing, but not to panic. She points out they are easy pitfalls for any writer. Even the most seasoned of writers must be reminded from time to time about certain aspects of their writing: i.e., thus the need for editors. This is a MUST HAVE for any writer's craft arsenal, along with its companion - Book I, *Show & Tell in a Nutshell: Demonstrated Transitions from Telling to Showing.* It would also be a fabulous gift for any high school or college student."

"I'm 100% sure this book is useful to any English native-speaker, but not being an English native-speaker, this book was even more useful to me, a real treasure. The English language is "wealthy", but we get so used to the same words and expressions that we miss the chance to bring more color and art to our Writing. The examples selected by the author encompass most adverbs and clichés in use. Her suggestions/alternatives are simply brilliant, even poetic in some cases. I wish I could describe things in such beautiful and clever way like her! But that's why I bought this book. I'm motivated enough to pimp my prose now! I definitely recommend it."

"If you're having trouble subverting adverbs and clichés, Jessica suggests using strong verbs for action and playing around with similes and metaphors when you're trying to convey emotion. This is great advice. Included is an index of commonly used adverbs and clichés to avoid! I also discovered an added bonus that I'm not sure the author intended—one of the writing prompts inspired a short story! Even if you aren't having trouble with adverbs and clichés, the exercises are bound to inspire good writing and creativity!"

"If you want adverbs and clichés simplified and portrayed in ways that make complete sense, add this pocket book to your shelf. In fact, even if you aren't sure that you need this book, get it anyway. It'll teach you something about your own writing as well as how to critique others."

Made in the USA
Lexington, KY
02 April 2014